<h1 style="text-align:center">TURKMENISTAN 2016 HUMAN RIGHTS REPORT</h1>

EXECUTIVE SUMMARY

Although the 2016 constitution declares Turkmenistan to be a secular democracy, the country has an authoritarian government controlled by the president, Gurbanguly Berdimuhamedov, and his inner circle. Berdimuhamedov has been president since 2006 and remained president following a February 2012 election the Organization for Security and Cooperation in Europe's (OSCE) Office of Democratic Institutions and Human Rights determined involved limited choice between competing political alternatives. In August the country conducted interim parliamentary elections, which were not subject to international observation, to fill a limited number of vacant seats. In September parliament ratified a new constitution that extended the presidential term in office from five to seven years, cancelled a maximum age limit of 70 years, and failed to reintroduce earlier term limits.

Civilian authorities maintained effective control over the security forces.

The most important human rights problems were: arbitrary arrest and detention; involuntary confinement; torture; disregard for civil liberties, including restrictions on freedoms of religion, speech, press, assembly, and movement; and citizens' inability to choose their government through free-and-fair elections that include real political alternatives.

Other continuing human rights problems included denial of due process and fair trial and arbitrary interference with privacy, home, and correspondence. Restrictions on access to the internet and certain sites and information sources remained a significant problem. There was also discrimination and violence against women; trafficking in persons, including use of government-compelled forced labor during the annual cotton harvest; restrictions on the free association of workers; and forced destruction of domiciles of Ashgabat residents.

Officials in the security services and elsewhere in the government acted with impunity. There were no reported prosecutions of government officials for human rights abuses.

Section 1. Respect for the Integrity of the Person, Including Freedom from:

a. Arbitrary Deprivation of Life and other Unlawful or Politically Motivated Killings

There were no reports the government or its agents committed arbitrary or unlawful killings, although Human Rights Watch (HRW) reported Altymurad Annamuradov, brother of exiled dissident journalist Chary Annamuradov, died September 4 after being kidnapped from his home and beaten by unknown persons. There were no reports of killings by narcotics traffickers or similar criminal groups.

b. Disappearance

There were no reports of new politically motivated disappearances during the year. A nongovernmental organization (NGO)-led advocacy campaign called "Prove They Are Alive!" maintained a list of disappeared prisoners; there were 87 on the list at year's end, although opposition media reported two of the prisoners died during the year. The list includes political dissident Gulgeldy Annaniyazov, former minister of foreign affairs Boris Shikhmuradov, and many others accused of participation in an alleged 2002 assassination attempt on former president Saparmurat Niyazov.

c. Torture and Other Cruel, Inhuman, or Degrading Treatment or Punishment

Although the constitution and law prohibit mistreatment, Amnesty International (AI) continued to report security officials tortured and beat criminal suspects, prisoners, and individuals deemed critical of the government to extract confessions and as a form of punishment. According to AI, law enforcement agencies used forms of torture, including pulling the genitals with pliers, electric shocks, and beatings with chair legs and plastic bottles filled with water.

The law requires the government to protect the health and lives of members of the armed forces. Members of the military reported, however, that hazing of conscripts continued and involved violations of human dignity, including brutality. During the year there were no confirmed reports of hazing deaths among conscripts, although external-based opposition news outlet *Alternative News of Turkmenistan (ANT)* reported a cadet died at a military institute due to hazing. Members of the military reported officers responded to cases of abuse, inspected conscripts for signs of abuse, and punished abusers in some cases. Hazing of conscripts reportedly was more prevalent outside of Ashgabat.

ANT also reported, in May, Unida Jumbayeva suffered an acid attack by unidentified assailants in Dashoguz city in retaliation for her complaints to the Ministry of Defense regarding alleged mistreatment of her son during his military conscription.

Prison and Detention Center Conditions

Prison conditions were generally unsanitary, overcrowded, harsh, and in some cases life threatening; however, facilities visited by representatives of the diplomatic corps in Bayram Ali juvenile detention center and Dashoguz women's prison, appeared more satisfactory. Some facilities, such as minimum security camp LBK-12 in Lebap Province, were in areas where inmates experienced extremely harsh climate conditions, with excessive heat in summer and frigid temperatures in winter. There were unconfirmed reports of physical abuse of prisoners by prison officials and other prisoners.

<u>Physical Conditions</u>: Official data on the average sentence or numbers of prisoners, including incarcerated juveniles, were not available. Persons in pretrial detention facilities were predominantly those sentenced but not yet transferred to penal colonies. The six pretrial detention facilities reportedly were designed for 1,120 persons but likely held many times that number.

The BLD-4 pretrial detention facility in Balkan Province, under the jurisdiction of the Ministry of Internal Affairs, reportedly held adults and juveniles together and included persons in pretrial detention, on remand, and those already convicted but not transferred to penal colonies.

Diseases, particularly tuberculosis (TB), were widespread in prisons. There were reports that due to overcrowding, officials held inmates diagnosed with TB and skin diseases with healthy detainees, contributing to the spread of disease. Nonetheless, a representative of an international organization reported that at least in and around Ashgabat, authorities held inmates with TB separately from healthy detainees. The Ministry of Internal Affairs reported in the past that inmates with TB were held separately from healthy inmates at the Dashoguz women's prison. There continued to be concerns the government did not adequately test and treat prisoners with TB before they returned to the general population, despite government claims to the contrary. The *ANT* news outlet reported prison authorities were ordered to report a 65 percent decrease in TB infection and declared infected prisoners to be healthy. In the past the government reported it transferred male prisoners diagnosed with TB to a special Ministry of Internal Affairs hospital in Mary Province for treatment and arranged for continuing treatment for released prisoners at their residences. There were also reports of high rates of cardiovascular disease.

The nutritional value of prison food was generally poor, and some prisoners suffered from malnutrition. Prisoners depended on relatives to supplement inadequate prison food. Some family members and inmates stated prison officials occasionally confiscated food parcels. It was not possible to determine whether potable water was available.

Administration: According to relatives, prison authorities denied food, medical, and other supplies brought by family members to some prisoners; sometimes denied family members access to prisoners; and did not make religious facilities available to all prisoners. The government allowed foreign diplomats to access nationals of their countries in detention facing criminal charges. The government did not provide information on prison recordkeeping, whether prisoners were permitted religious observance, or on systematic monitoring of prison and detention center conditions. Alternatives to sentencing for nonviolent offenders included suspended sentences, fines, and garnishment of wages. The government did not confirm whether it established a prison ombudsman.

Independent Monitoring: During the year government officials allowed members of the diplomatic corps to visit the Bayram Ali juvenile detention center in Mary Province. The government allowed members of the diplomatic corps to visit the women's prison in Dashoguz in 2015. In both cases it was not clear whether the conditions of the prison were authentic. Outside of individual consular visits, there were no other prison visits by the diplomatic community. The International Committee of the Red Cross reported minimal prison access in 2012-13 but stated the access granted did not meet its basic visit access standards. The diplomatic community requested, but was not granted, access to the adult prison near Owadan Depe.

Improvements: There were reports treatment of prisoners and food quality improved in correctional facilities in Ahal, Lebap, and Mary Provinces.

d. Arbitrary Arrest or Detention

The law prohibits arbitrary arrest and detention, but both remained serious problems.

Role of the Police and Security Apparatus

The Ministry of Internal Affairs directs the criminal police, which works closely with the Ministry of National Security on matters of national safety and security. The security ministry plays a role in personnel changes in other ministries, often dictating assignments, and enforces presidential decrees. There were continued reports both the security ministry and criminal police operated with impunity in the prosecution of criminal cases and in the harassment of unregistered religious groups and persons perceived to be critical of the regime. No information was available on whether the presidential commission created in 2007 to review citizen complaints of abuse had conducted any inquiries that resulted in accountability of any members of the security forces for abuses. There was no national strategy to reform the police or security apparatus.

Arrest Procedures and Treatment of Detainees

A warrant is not required for arrest when officials catch a suspect in the act of committing an offense. The prosecutor general must issue an authorization for arrest within 72 hours of detention. If investigating authorities do not find evidence of guilt and issue a formal indictment within 10 days of detention, they must release the detainee; however, authorities did not always comply with this requirement. If they find evidence, an investigation may last as long as two months. A provincial- or national-level prosecutor may extend the investigation period to six months. The national prosecutor general or deputy prosecutor general may extend the investigation period to a maximum of one year. Following the investigation, the prosecutor prepares a bill of indictment and transfers the case to the court. Courts generally followed these procedures, and the prosecutor promptly informs detainees of the charges against them.

The criminal procedure code provides for a bail system and surety; however, authorities did not implement these provisions. The law entitles detainees to immediate access to an attorney of their choice after a formal accusation. For a number of reasons, however, detainees may not have had prompt or regular access to legal counsel--they may have been unaware of the law; security forces may have ignored the entitlement to counsel; or the practice of seeking formal legal counsel was not a cultural norm. Authorities denied some detainees visits by family members during the year. Families sometimes did not know the whereabouts of detained relatives. Incommunicado detention was a problem. The extent to which authorities failed to protect due process in the criminal justice system was unclear.

<u>Arbitrary Arrest</u>: The law characterizes any opposition to the government as treason. Persons convicted of treason faced life imprisonment and were ineligible for pardoning. In the past the government arrested and filed charges on economic or criminal grounds against those expressing critical or differing views instead of charging its critics with treason.

There were reports of arbitrary arrests and detentions. Authorities frequently singled out human rights activists, journalists, members of religious groups, ethnic minorities, and dissidents, as well as members of NGOs who interacted with foreigners.

Jehovah's Witnesses reported police officers disrupted a group of followers gathered illegally in a private apartment in Turkmenabat by breaking into the apartment through its balcony. Police assaulted some members of the group and all were detained. The police later released the detainees without charge, with the exception of one who remained in detention for 15 days. Unregistered religious groups are not allowed to meet according to Turkmenistan's religion law adopted in April.

Forum 18 reported the antinarcotics service detained and questioned four Baptists after seizing their religious literature, cell phones, and money. They were later fined 500 manat ($143) for possession of illegal religious literature.

According to Forum 18, member of Jehovah's Witnesses Mansur Masharipov received a one-year sentence for allegedly assaulting a police officer following his 2014 detention after police raided his home and confiscated religious material. Masharipov was appealing his conviction.

Mansur Mingelov, an activist for the rights of Balochi minorities, has remained in prison since his arrest in 2012. According to AI reports, he conducted a hunger strike in 2014 in an attempt to have his case reviewed. The authorities reportedly reviewed his case but did not release him.

<u>Pretrial Detention</u>: In most cases the law permits detention of no more than two months, but in exceptional cases, it may be extended to one year with approval of the prosecutor general. For minor crimes a much shorter investigation period applies. Consistent with recent trends, authorities rarely exceeded legal limits for pretrial detention. In the past chronic corruption and cumbersome bureaucratic processes contributed to lengthy trial delays; however, the government's

anticorruption efforts and the establishment of the Academy of State Service to Improve State Employees' Qualifications generally eliminated such delays. Forced confessions also played a part in the reduction of time in pretrial detention. Accused persons are entitled to challenge the court, but were unlikely to do so for fear of retribution.

<u>Detainee's Ability to Challenge Lawfulness of Detention before a Court</u>: Persons arrested or detained are not entitled to challenge the legal basis or arbitrary nature of their detention while detained or obtain prompt release if unlawfully detained. There were no reports of prompt release or compensation of unlawfully detained persons. According to Turkmenistan's Criminal Code, law enforcement authorities may detain a person for 72 hours without charge. Persons arrested or detained unlawfully, however, may seek reimbursement for damages following release. Law enforcement authorities found guilty of unlawful detention or arrest may be punished by demotion or suspension for five years, correctional labor service for up to two years, and imprisonment for up to eight years.

e. Denial of Fair Public Trial

Although the law provides for an independent judiciary, the judiciary was controlled by and subordinate to the executive. There was no legislative review of the president's judicial appointments and dismissals. The president had sole authority to dismiss any judge. The judiciary was widely reputed to be corrupt and inefficient.

Trial Procedures

The law provides for due process for defendants, including a public trial; the right to attend the trial; access to accusatory material; the right to call witnesses; the right to a defense attorney, including a court-appointed lawyer if the defendant cannot afford one; and the right to represent oneself in court. Authorities, however, often denied these rights. Defendants frequently did not enjoy a presumption of innocence. The government permits the public to attend most trials, but it closed some, especially those considered politically sensitive. There were few independent lawyers available to represent defendants. The criminal procedure code provides that defendants be present at their trials and consult with their attorneys in a timely manner. The law sets no restrictions on a defendant's access to an attorney. The court at times did not allow defendants to confront or question a witness against them and denied defendants and their attorneys access to government evidence. In some cases courts refused to accept exculpatory evidence provided by defense attorneys, even if that evidence might have changed the outcome of the trial. Courts did not offer interpreters to defendants who did not speak Turkmen.

Even when the courts observed due process, the authority of the government prosecutor far exceeded that of the defense attorney, making it difficult for the defendant to receive a fair trial. Court transcripts frequently were flawed or incomplete, especially when there was a need to translate defendants' testimony from Russian to Turkmen. Defendants could appeal a lower court's decision and petition the president for clemency. There were credible reports that judges and prosecutors often predetermined the outcome of the trial and sentence.

Political Prisoners and Detainees

Opposition groups and some international organizations stated the government held political prisoners and detainees. The precise number of these persons, which included persons charged with involvement in the 2002 alleged attack on then president Niyazov, remained unknown. According to one international representative, however, the government asserted in 2014 it imprisoned 104 persons in the wake of the coup attempt and released 32. During the year external news outlets reported two of these prisoners died. Those convicted of treason faced life imprisonment and were ineligible for amnesty, although they could receive reductions of sentence from the president. The government denied that any of these persons were political prisoners.

Civil Judicial Procedures and Remedies

The civil judiciary system was neither independent nor impartial, as the president appointed all judges. According to the law, evidence gathered during a criminal investigation can serve as the basis for a civil action in a process called "civil lawsuit in criminal justice." In the past there were reports of bribes in the civil court system to ensure a particular outcome. In cases in which the state had interests regarding an individual citizen, it used the judiciary to impose court orders. The most commonly enforced court orders were eviction notices. Persons and organizations may appeal adverse decisions to regional human rights bodies, but local courts were unlikely to reverse decisions in light of successful appeals.

Property Restitution

The government failed to enforce the law consistently with respect to restitution or compensation for confiscation of private property. The government continued to demolish private homes as part of an urban renewal program without adequately compensating owners. Housing offered as compensation to displaced homeowners was often smaller than housing lost, because gardens and outbuildings surrounding a house were not considered "useful living space." There were credible reports some residents received no compensation. If housing offered as compensation had more living space than the demolished home, the displaced homeowner could be forced to pay up to 4,200 manat ($1,200) per square meter (10.7 square feet) for the additional space. Although a process existed for displaced homeowners to file complaints and appeals, it was not possible to determine how the process worked in practice.

f. Arbitrary or Unlawful Interference with Privacy, Family, Home, or Correspondence

The constitution and law prohibit such actions, but authorities frequently did not respect these prohibitions. Authorities reportedly searched private homes without judicial or other appropriate authorization.

The law does not regulate surveillance by the state security apparatus, which regularly monitored the activities of officials, citizens, opponents and critics of the government, and foreigners. Security officials used physical surveillance, telephone tapping, electronic eavesdropping, and informers. Authorities frequently queried the parents of students studying overseas and sometimes threatened state employees they would lose their jobs if they maintained friendships with foreigners.

The government reportedly intercepted surface mail before delivery, and letters and parcels taken to the post office had to remain unsealed for government inspection.

Persons harassed, detained, or arrested by authorities, as well as their family members, reported the government caused family members to be fired from their jobs or expelled from school. Authorities sometimes also detained and interrogated family members.

Section 2. Respect for Civil Liberties, Including:

a. Freedom of Speech and Press

The constitution provides for freedom of speech and press, but the government did not respect these rights.

<u>Freedom of Speech and Expression</u>: The law requires political parties to allow representatives of the Central Election Committee and Ministry of Justice to monitor their meetings. The government also warned critics against speaking with visiting journalists or other foreigners about human rights problems.

During the year the government publicized new laws that stipulate civil servants must refrain from public statements on the activities of the government and its leaders if such statements are not part of their official duties. The laws also state civil servants must refrain from making public statements regarding the value of goods, works, and services, including the government's budget, borrowing, or debt.

In October state police services threatened to harm animal rights activist Galina Kucherenko for her online postings protesting a government campaign to destroy stray dogs and cats found on the city streets. Their harassment and intimidation led to Kucherenko's two-month involuntary confinement to her home, which appeared to ease toward the end of the year.

<u>Press and Media Freedoms</u>: The government financed and controlled the publication of books and almost all other print media and online newspapers/journals. Quasi-independent weekly newspaper *Rysgal* continued to operate, although its stories were largely reprints from state media outlets or reflected the views of the state news agency. The government maintained restrictions on the importation of foreign newspapers except for the private, but government-sanctioned, Turkish newspaper *Zaman Turkmenistan*, which reflected the views of the official state newspapers, and *Atavatan-Turkmenistan*, a Turkish journal.

The government controlled radio and domestic television, but satellite dishes providing access to foreign television programming were widespread throughout the country. International organizations and news outlets highlighted the forced removal of some satellite dishes by the government and replacement with telecommunications packages, such as cable, that limited access to certain channels and kinds of information. Citizens also received international radio programs through satellite access.

The government continued its ban on subscriptions to foreign periodicals by nongovernmental entities, although copies of nonpolitical periodicals appeared occasionally in the bazaars. The government maintained a subscription service to Russian-language outlets for government workers, although these publications were not available for public use.

There was no independent oversight of media accreditation, no defined criteria for allocating press cards, no assured provision for receiving accreditation when space was available, and no protection against the withdrawal of accreditation for political reasons. The government required all foreign correspondents to apply for accreditation. It granted visas to journalists from outside the country only to cover specific events, such as international conferences and summit meetings, where it could monitor their activities. The government reported 25 foreign mass media agencies, such as *Xinhua*, the *Associated Press*, *RIA Novosti*, and *Turkish TRT*, were accredited and that *Trend*, *AZERTAC*, and the *Associated Press of Pakistan* applied for accreditation. The government did not respond to a November 2015 call by the international community for accreditation of Radio Free Europe/Radio Liberty (RFE/RL).

Violence and Harassment: The government subjected journalists critical of its official policy to surveillance and harassment. There were reports law enforcement officials harassed and monitored citizen journalists who worked for foreign media outlets, including by monitoring their telephone conversations and restricting their travel abroad. RFE/RL stringer Saparmamed Nepeskuliyev was arrested, charged, and convicted for possession of narcotics and sentenced to three years' incarceration in 2015. He remained imprisoned. HRW disputed the legal basis of the charge, stating it was politically motivated. Visiting foreign journalists reported harassment and denial of freedom of movement when they attempted to report from the country.

Several RFE/RL stringers faced harassment and intimidation throughout the year. On October 25, unknown persons attacked and robbed Soltan Achilova after police confronted her for photographing a line of persons queuing for cigarettes at a convenience store. Achilova was harassed verbally by unknown persons on November 14 and was struck by men on bicycles on November 25.

RFE/RL stringer Khudayberdy Allashov was arrested and detained in Konye-Urgench December 3 for possession of an illegal local tobacco product. Reportedly, police also beat Allashov following his arrest, detained his wife and mother, and seized his mother's home. Allashov faced a seven-year sentence for the alleged crime and remained in jail at year's end.

The OSCE reported in December RFE/RL stringer Rovshen Yazmuhamedov was threatened by authorities with enforcement of a previously suspended jail sentence. As in previous years, the government required journalists working for state-owned media to obtain permission to cover specific events as well as to publish or broadcast the subject matter they covered.

Censorship or Content Restrictions: The law prohibits censorship and provides for freedom to gather and disseminate information, but authorities did not implement the law. The government continued to censor newspapers and prohibit reporting of opposition political views or any criticism of the president. Domestic journalists and foreign news correspondents often engaged in self-censorship due to fear of government reprisal.

To regulate domestic printing and copying activities, the government required all publishing houses and printing and photocopying establishments to register their equipment. The government did not allow the publication of works on topics that were out of favor with the government, including some works of fiction.

Internet Freedom

The government continued to monitor citizens' e-mail and internet activity. Reports indicated the Ministry of National Security controlled the main access gateway and that several servers belonging to internet protocol addresses registered to the Ministry of Communications operated software that allowed the government to record Voice over Internet Protocol (VOIP) conversations, turn on computer cameras and microphones, and log keystrokes. The authorities blocked access to websites they considered sensitive, including YouTube, Twitter, and Facebook, as well as virtual private network connections, including those of diplomatic missions and international businesses, and severely restricted internet access to other websites. Skype, an encrypted VOIP service, was blocked throughout the year.

According to the government, 12 percent of the population used the internet. The percentage of the population that accessed the internet via cell phones reportedly was significantly higher, although official estimates were not available. Much of the population received its news from Russian- and Turkish-language cable and satellite television feeds.

Academic Freedom and Cultural Events

The government did not tolerate criticism of government policy or the president in academic circles and curtailed research in areas it considered politically sensitive, such as comparative law, history, ethnic relations, and theology. In 2015 a presidential decree established procedures for the government to certify foreign diplomas. To have foreign diplomas formally recognized, graduates must complete an application, submit information on their family history for three generations, and pass regular Turkmen university graduation exams related to their majors. Due to this extensive process, many graduates of foreign universities reported they were unable to certify their diplomas with authorities at the Ministry of Education, making them ineligible for employment at state agencies. Some graduates reported ministry officials demanded bribes to allow certification of their diplomas. The government strictly controlled the production of plays and performances in state theaters, and these were severely limited. Authorities also strictly controlled film screenings and limited viewings to approved films dubbed or subtitled in Turkmen and Russian, unless sponsored by a foreign embassy.

The Ministry of Culture censored and monitored all public exhibitions, including music, art, and cultural events.

b. Freedom of Peaceful Assembly and Association

Freedom of Assembly

The constitution and law provide for freedom of assembly, but the government restricted this right. During the year authorities neither granted the required permits for public meetings and demonstrations nor allowed unregistered organizations to hold demonstrations. In some instances religious groups reported their members were arrested while gathering for private dinners.

Freedom of Association

Although the constitution and law provide for freedom of association, the government restricted this right. The law requires all NGOs to register with the Ministry of Justice and all foreign assistance to be coordinated through the Ministry of Foreign Affairs. Unregistered NGO activity is punishable by a fine, short-term detention, and confiscation of property.

Of the estimated 109 registered NGOs, international organizations recognized only a few as independent. NGOs reported the government presented a number of administrative obstacles to NGOs that attempted to register. Authorities reportedly rejected some applications repeatedly on technical grounds. In 2014 the government reported it registered three NGOs whose primary focus was sports and leisure activities. Some organizations awaiting registration found alternate ways to carry out activities, such as registering as businesses or subsidiaries of other registered groups, but others temporarily suspended or limited their activities. Although the law states there is a process for registering foreign assistance, NGOs had difficulty registering bilateral foreign assistance in practice due to a 2013 decree requiring such registration.

Sources noted a number of barriers to the formation and functioning of civil society. These included regulations that permitted the Ministry of Justice to send representatives to association events and meetings and requirements that associations notify the government about their planned activities.

c. Freedom of Religion

See the Department of State's *International Religious Freedom Report* at www.state.gov/religiousfreedomreport/.

d. Freedom of Movement, Internally Displaced Persons, Protection of Refugees, and Stateless Persons

The constitution and law do not provide for full freedom of movement.

In-country Movement: The law requires internal passports and residency permits. Persons residing or working without residency permits face forcible removal to their place of registration. A requirement for a border permit remained in effect for all foreigners wishing to travel to border areas.

The law does not permit dual citizenship, and in 2015 the government terminated an agreement with Russia that previously provided an exception for certain dual Turkmen-Russian citizens. All dual citizens are obliged to renounce one of their citizenships if they want to travel outside the country. The process of renouncing Turkmen citizenship is not transparent and can take up to a year.

Foreign Travel: The government continued to bar certain citizens from departing under its Law on Migration. The law states that citizens of Turkmenistan may be denied exit from Turkmenistan "if their exit contravenes the interests of national security of Turkmenistan." "Prove They Are Alive!" reported that any of the country's law enforcement bodies can initiate a travel ban on a citizen and that travelers in various categories may be denied departure, including: young men obliged to military service, persons facing criminal and civil charges or under probationary sentence, relatives of persons reportedly connected and imprisoned for the 2002 alleged assassination attempt, as well as journalists, civil society activists, and their family members. Although the government denied maintaining a "black list" of local persons not permitted to travel abroad, *ANT* reported that such a list existed and contained approximately 17,000 names. According to various sources, in most cases, travelers who were stopped were not given an explanation for denial of departure and were only informed of the ban upon attempting foreign travel from the airport. Some individuals were able to obtain documentation from the State Migration Service later stating they were not allowed to depart the country, but without justification for the ban. In some cases authorities initially denied travelers departure from the country, but after several days, or in some cases weeks, the travelers were allowed to depart without explanation for the delay.

During the year the government allowed some persons previously banned from travel to depart the country. For instance, family members of emigrant opposition politician Pirimguly Tanrykuliev were allowed to depart the country after previously being informed they were banned from departing the country for life.

The government routinely prevented citizens from travelling abroad for programs sponsored by foreign governments, unless the program was specifically approved in advance by the foreign ministry. Migration officials often stopped "nonapproved" travelers at the airport and prevented them from leaving. In some cases, however, those traveling for approved programs were also not allowed to depart or were delayed.

The Law on Migration provides for restrictions on travel by citizens who have had access to state secrets, presented falsified personal information, committed a serious crime, were under surveillance, might become victims of trafficking, previously violated the law of the destination country, or whose travel contradicts the interests of national security. In some cases the law provides for time limits on the travel ban as well as fines for its infraction. Former public-sector employees who had access to state secrets were prevented from traveling abroad for five years after terminating their employment with the government. The law allows authorities to forbid recipients of presidential amnesties from traveling abroad for a period of up to two years. The law also allows the government to impose limitations on obtaining education in specific professions and specialties.

Exile: The law provides for internal exile, requiring persons to reside in a certain area for a fixed term of two to five years.

Protection of Refugees

While formally there is a system for granting refugee status, it was inactive. In 2009 the government assumed responsibility from the UN High Commissioner for Refugees (UNHCR) for making refugee status determinations but has not granted refugee status since. UNHCR had observer status at government-run refugee-status determination hearings. Persons determined by the government not to be refugees obtained mandate refugee status from UNHCR. Mandate refugees were required to renew UNHCR certificates with the government annually. In 2015 UNHCR reported that 27 UNHCR mandate refugees resided in the country, but it provided no updates for 2016. The country did not grant citizenship to any UNHCR mandate refugees during the year.

In 2014 the government amended the Law on Migration to permit refugees to receive, at no charge, biometric identification and travel documents compliant with the requirements of the International Civil Aviation Organization.

Access to Asylum: The laws provide for the granting of asylum or refugee status, and the government has established a system for providing protection to refugees. The country has not granted asylum since 2005.

Stateless Persons

The country had a significant population of former Soviet Union citizens who became stateless due to the breakup of the Soviet Union. In December 2015 UNHCR estimated there were 7,111 stateless persons or persons of underdetermined nationality in the country. The number of stateless persons who were also refugees was not available. Citizenship is derived primarily from one's parents. The requirement that applicants for citizenship prove they are not citizens of another country impeded efforts to establish the nationality of undocumented persons. According to UNHCR, however, in the past 10 years, the government granted citizenship to an estimated 18,000 stateless persons. During the year the government granted citizenship to 1,381 stateless persons residing in the country. In 2014 the government amended its Law on Migration to allow stateless persons to reside in the country legally and travel internationally with government-issued identification and travel documents.

Undocumented stateless persons did not have access to public benefits, education, or employment opportunities.

Section 3. Freedom to Participate in the Political Process

Despite a constitutional provision giving citizens the ability to choose their government in periodic elections based on universal and equal suffrage, there have not been free-and-fair elections in Turkmenistan. There was no bona fide political opposition to the president, and alternative candidates came from derivative party structures, such as the state-controlled Union of Industrialists and Entrepreneurs, or are members of individual initiative groups. Elections were conducted by secret ballot. The constitution declares the country to be a secular democracy in the form of a presidential republic. It calls for separation of powers among the branches of government but vests a disproportionate share of power in the presidency. The president's power over the state continued to be nearly absolute. According to the OSCE, the election law does not meet OSCE standards.

Elections and Political Participation

In September parliament ratified a new constitution that extended the presidential term in office from five to seven years, repealed a maximum age limit of 70 years, and failed to reinstitute term limits for the presidency.

Recent Elections: A presidential election took place in 2012; however, the OSCE determined conditions were not appropriate for an observer mission. The OSCE's Office of Democratic Institutions and Human Rights (ODIHR) noted in its 2011 *Needs Assessment Mission Report* that the deployment of an observer mission would not add value to the election due to limitations on fundamental freedoms, the absence of political pluralism, and the lack of progress in bringing the country's legal framework in line with OSCE commitments for democratic elections. The government did not invite the OSCE to send observers, but the Commonwealth of Independent States (CIS), which the country chaired in 2012, sent a small observer mission that did not have unrestricted access to polling stations and did not release a comprehensive observation report.

In 2013 the government enacted an electoral code that governs the activities of the Central Election Committee, defines the rights of voters, and establishes election procedures.

In 2013 the government held national parliamentary elections, and for the first time, a second political party, the Party of Industrialists and Entrepreneurs, competed for seats on a national scale. The government invited the OSCE to send observers for the elections. While the 2013 report of ODIHR's needs assessment mission did not recommend the deployment of an election-monitoring mission, the ODIHR sent a 15-member election-assessment mission to review further the new legal and administrative framework for elections. The final report of ODIHR's mission noted the elections took place in a strictly controlled political environment characterized by a lack of respect for fundamental freedoms. The report noted also that, despite the existence of a second political party, voters did not have a genuine choice between political alternatives. The OSCE Parliamentary Assembly also sent a 12-member election-assessment team with eight European parliamentarians, while the CIS sent 68 observers from nine countries. In August local council elections took place but were not monitored by independent observer groups.

During the year the government conducted elections to fill parliamentary vacancies in conjunction with local government elections. The government did not invite observers, and all newly elected members of parliament represented progovernment parties. The government's Central Election Committee reported the elections were conducted consistent with international standards.

<u>Political Parties and Political Participation</u>: The law makes it extremely difficult for genuinely independent political parties to organize, nominate candidates, and campaign, since it grants the Ministry of Justice broad powers over the registration process and the authority to monitor party meetings. The law prohibits political parties based on religion, region, or profession as well as parties that "offend moral norms." The law does not explain how a party can appeal its closure by the government. The law permits public associations and organizations to put forth candidates for elected office. State media covered the activities of President Berdimuhamedov, the Democratic Party, the Party of Industrialists and Entrepreneurs, the Agrarian Party, and trade and professional unions.

There were neither organized opposition nor independent political groups operating in the country. The three registered political parties were the ruling Democratic Party (the former Communist Party), the Party of Industrialists and Entrepreneurs, and the Agrarian Party. Each of these parties, which were progovernment in orientation, nominated a candidate for anticipated February 2017 presidential elections. Initiative groups put forward six additional candidates who are running in their individual capacities. The government did not officially prohibit membership in other political organizations, but there were no reports of persons who claimed membership in political organizations other than these three parties and a smattering of representatives of individual initiative groups. Authorities did not allow opposition movements based abroad--including the National Democratic Movement of Turkmenistan, the Republican Party of Turkmenistan, and the Fatherland (Watan) Party--to operate within the country.

Participation of Women and Minorities: Women served in prominent government positions, including as speaker of parliament, but only one woman served in the 10-member Cabinet of Ministers. The government gave preference for appointed government positions to ethnic Turkmen, but ethnic minorities occupied some senior government positions. Members of the president's Ahal-Teke tribe, the largest in the country, held the most prominent roles in cultural and political life.

Section 4. Corruption and Lack of Transparency in Government

While the law provides criminal penalties for official corruption, the government did not implement the law effectively, and officials reportedly often engaged in corrupt practices with impunity. Corruption existed in the security forces and in all social and economic sectors. Factors encouraging corruption included the existence of patronage networks, low government salaries that in the latter half of the year were paid as much as three months behind schedule, a lack of fiscal transparency and accountability, the absence of published macroeconomic data, and the fear of government retaliation against citizens who choose to highlight corrupt acts. According to Freedom House and the World Bank's Worldwide Governance Indicators, the country had a severe corruption problem.

Corruption: One regional governor, one deputy minister, and two deputy chairmen of the Cabinet of Ministers were dismissed from their positions during the year over allegations of corruption.

Financial Disclosure: The law does not require elected or appointed officials to disclose their incomes or assets. Financial disclosure requirements are neither transparent nor consistent with international norms. Government enterprises are not required to publicize financial statements, even to foreign partners. Local auditors, not internationally recognized firms, often conducted financial audits.

<u>Public Access to Information</u>: Although the Law on Mass Media allows for public access to government information if requested through accredited mass media sources, the government did not provide such access. Authorities denied requests for specific information on the grounds that the information was a state secret. Most statistical data were considered state secrets, including detailed government budget data, macroeconomic figures, and the status of financial reserves. There was no public disclosure of demographic data, and officials published manipulated economic and financial data to justify state policies and expenditures.

Section 5. Governmental Attitude Regarding International and Nongovernmental Investigation of Alleged Violations of Human Rights

There were no domestic human rights NGOs due to the government's refusal to register such organizations and restrictions that made activity by unregistered organizations illegal. The government continued to monitor the activities of nonpolitical social and cultural organizations.

<u>The United Nations or Other International Bodies</u>: There were no international human rights NGOs with a permanent presence in the country, although the government permitted international organizations, including the OSCE and UNHCR, to have resident missions. The government permitted the OSCE to conduct workshops and study tours on prisoners' rights, women's rights, religious freedom, and media freedom. The government collaborated with the International Organization for Migration and UNHCR on migration and statelessness issues. Government restrictions on freedoms of speech, press, and association severely restricted international organizations' ability to investigate, understand, and fully evaluate the government's human rights policies and practices.

The government allowed unfettered access to the OSCE Center. There were no reports that the government discouraged citizens from contacting other international organizations.

<u>Government Human Rights Bodies</u>: The government-run National Institute for Democracy and Human Rights is not an independent body, and its ability to obtain redress for citizens was limited. The institute, established in 1996 with a mandate to support democratization and monitor the protection of human rights, played an unofficial ombudsman's role in resolving some petitions citizens submitted through the institute's complaints committee. The Interagency Commission on Enforcing Turkmenistan's International Obligations on Human Rights and International Humanitarian Law meets biannually to coordinate the

implementation of a limited number of recommendations from international human rights bodies. The parliamentary Committee on the Protection of Human Rights and Liberties oversees human rights-related legislation, and during the year it worked with the UN Development Program to draft the country's National Action Plan for Human Rights.

The country's new constitution, approved in September, established a human rights ombudsman. Secondary legislation adopted in November stated the ombudsman must be nominated by the president and confirmed by parliament. The law empowers the ombudsman to receive and review human rights violations reported by citizens and confirm or deny the violation and advise the complainant regarding legal redress. The ombudsman is obliged to submit an annual human rights report to the president and parliament, which shall be published and distributed via local media. The ombudsman enjoys legal immunity and cannot be prosecuted, arrested, or detained for his official acts while in office. By year's end President Berdimuhamedov had not nominated a candidate for ombudsman.

Section 6. Discrimination, Societal Abuses, and Trafficking in Persons

Women

Rape and Domestic Violence: The law criminalizes rape, and penalties range from three to 10 years in prison. Rape of a victim under 14 years of age is punishable by 10 to 25 years in prison. A cultural bias against reporting or acknowledging rape made it difficult to determine the extent of the problem. The law prohibits domestic violence, including spousal abuse, through provisions in the criminal code that address intentional infliction of injury. Penalties range from fines to 15 years in prison, based on the extent of the injury, although enforcement of the law varied.

Anecdotal reports indicated domestic violence against women was common; most victims of domestic violence kept silent because they were unaware of their rights or afraid of increased violence from husbands and relatives. NGO Keik Okara maintained a shelter for victims of domestic violence that was supported by the OSCE. Keik Okara continued to operate a domestic violence hotline and provided free legal consultations and psychological assistance to victims of domestic violence. The NGO also organized awareness-raising seminars on domestic violence. One official women's group in Ashgabat and several informal groups in other regions assisted victims of domestic violence.

Sexual Harassment: No law specifically prohibits sexual harassment, and reports suggested sexual harassment existed in the workplace.

Reproductive Rights: Persons have the right to decide freely and responsibly the number, spacing, and timing of their children; manage their reproductive health; and have access to the information and means to do so, free from discrimination, coercion, or violence. Some married women opposed the use of contraception. According to the UN Population Fund, however, during the year there was a 15 percent unmet need for women who wanted but did not have access to a modern method of family planning.

Discrimination: By law women have full legal equality with men, including equal pay, access to loans, the ability to start and own a business, and access to government jobs. Nevertheless, women continued to experience discrimination due to cultural biases, and some of these laws were not consistently enforced. Some employers allegedly gave preference to men to avoid losing employees due to pregnancy or child-care responsibilities. Women were underrepresented in the upper levels of government-owned economic enterprises and were concentrated in the health-care, education, and service professions. The government restricted women from working in some dangerous and environmentally unsafe jobs. The government did not acknowledge, address, or report on discrimination against women. There were no reports of discrimination in areas such as marriage, divorce, and child custody.

Children

Birth Registration: By law a child derives citizenship from his/her parents. A child born to stateless persons possessing permanent resident status in the country is also a citizen.

From 2010 to 2015, according to the UN Children's Fund (UNICEF) *State of the World's Children* report, 96 percent of children had their births registered.

Education: Education was free, compulsory, and universal through grades 10 or 11, depending on what year a child started school. There were reports that, in some rural communities, parents removed girls from school as young as age nine to work at home.

Child Abuse: In 2015 the UN Committee on the Rights of the Child called on the government to improve by 2020 its collection of data on children's rights, remove restrictions on civil society organizations working on children's rights, guarantee children's access to internet and international media, create a mechanism to which children deprived of liberty in all areas can address complaints, consider creation of a centralized system for registration of adoptions, and ratify the Optional Protocol of the Convention of the Rights of the Child. The country had not approved a national action plan for children's rights. The government did not provide substantive answers to the UN committee's previous requests for updated information about mechanisms for protecting children in vulnerable situations from discrimination, the implementation of measures prohibiting corporal punishment, children's access to potable water and adequate sanitation, and what had been done to improve the quality of education for children.

Early and Forced Marriage: The legal minimum age for marriage is 18. According to UNICEF's 2014 report, *State of the World's Children*, 7 percent of marriages involved minors.

Sexual Exploitation of Children: The legal age of consent is 16. The law forbids the production of pornographic materials or objects for distribution, as well as the advertisement or trade in text, movies or videos, graphics, or other objects of a pornographic nature, including those involving children. An Interpol report noted the criminal code "enacts criminal liability for involvement of minors into prostitution."

International Child Abductions: The country is a party to the 1980 Hague Convention on the Civil Aspects of International Child Abduction. See the Department of State's *Annual Report on International Parental Child Abduction* at travel.state.gov/content/childabduction/en/legal/compliance.html.

Anti-Semitism

There were an estimated 200-250 Jews, mainly in Ashgabat, but there was no organized Jewish community. Human rights advocacy organization Crude Accountability reported several instances of anti-Semitic language on online pro-government news portals and in comment sections of online opposition news sources in reference to civil society activists and opposition journalists.

Trafficking in Persons

See the Department of State's *Trafficking in Persons Report* at www.state.gov/j/tip/rls/tiprpt/.

Persons with Disabilities

The law prohibits discrimination against persons with physical, sensory, intellectual, and mental disabilities in employment, education, access to health care, and the provision of state services in other areas. Despite the law, persons with disabilities encountered discrimination and denial of work, education, and access to health care and other state services because of strong cultural biases.

The government provided subsidies and pensions for persons with disabilities, but the assistance was inadequate to meet basic needs. The government considered persons with disabilities who received subsidies as being employed and therefore ineligible to compete for jobs in the government, the country's largest employer.

Some students with disabilities were unable to obtain education because there were no qualified teachers, and facilities were not accessible for persons with disabilities. Although the law requires universities to provide specialized entrance exams to applicants with disabilities, students with disabilities experienced difficulties in gaining admission to universities. The government placed children with disabilities, including those with mental disabilities, in boarding schools where they were to receive education and, if able to work, employment. In practice, however, the schools provided neither. Special schools for those with sensory disabilities existed in the larger cities. Boarding schools with rehabilitation centers for persons with disabilities existed in each province and in Ashgabat. The government operated six combined education and rehabilitation centers, one in each of the five provinces and one in the capital. Each center was designed to serve 420 students with disabilities.

Although the law requires new construction projects to include facilities that allow access by persons with disabilities, compliance was inconsistent and older buildings remained inaccessible. A lack of consistent accessibility standards resulted in some new buildings with inappropriately designed access ramps. The Ministry of Social Welfare is responsible for protecting the rights of persons with disabilities. The ministry provided venues and organizational support for activities conducted by NGOs that assist persons with disabilities. The law provides for the right to vote for all, including for persons with disabilities.

National/Racial/Ethnic Minorities

The law provides for equal rights and freedoms for all citizens. Minority groups tried to register as NGOs to have legal status to conduct cultural events, but no minority group succeeded in registering during the year.

The law designates Turkmen as the official language, although it also provides for the rights of speakers of minority languages. Russian remained prevalent in commerce and everyday life in the capital, even as the government continued its campaign to conduct official business solely in Turkmen. The government required ministry employees to pass tests demonstrating knowledge of professional subjects in Turkmen, and the government dismissed those employees who failed the examination. The government dedicated resources to provide Turkmen instruction for non-Turkmen speakers only in primary and secondary schools.

Non-Turkmen speakers in government noted that some avenues for promotion and job advancement were not available to them, and only a handful of non-Turkmen occupied high-level jobs in government. In some cases applicants for government jobs had to provide information about their ethnicity going back three generations. Because the government often targeted non-Turkmen first for dismissal when government layoffs occurred, disproportionately few non-Turkmen held government positions.

Acts of Violence, Discrimination, and Other Abuses Based on Sexual Orientation and Gender Identity

Sexual contact between men is illegal under a section of the criminal code on pederasty, with punishment of up to two years in prison and the possible imposition of an additional two- to five-year term in a labor camp. The law also stipulates sentences of up to 20 years for repeated acts of pederasty, homosexual acts with juveniles, or the spread of HIV or other sexually transmitted infections through same-sex contact. The law does not mention same-sex sexual contact between women. Enforcement of the law was selective. Antidiscrimination laws do not apply to lesbian, gay, bisexual, transgender, and intersex (LGBTI) persons. Society does not accept transgender individuals, and the government provided no legal protection or recognition of their gender identity.

There were reports of detention, threats, and other abuses based on sexual orientation and gender identity. No official information was available regarding discrimination against LGBTI individuals in employment, housing, statelessness, access to education, or health care. Since same-sex sexual activity and nonconforming gender identity were taboo subjects in the country's traditional society, observers noted social stigma prevented reporting of incidents.

Other Societal Violence or Discrimination

There were reports of discrimination and violence against some religious minority groups, many of which the government officially referred to as "sects," including Jehovah's Witnesses. The government generally perpetrated or condoned these actions.

Section 7. Worker Rights

a. Freedom of Association and the Right to Collective Bargaining

The law provides for the right of workers to form and join independent unions and to bargain collectively with their employers. The law prohibits workers from striking. The law does not prohibit anti-union discrimination against union members and organizers. There are no mechanisms for resolving complaints of discrimination, nor does the law provide for reinstatement of workers fired for anti-union activity.

The government did not respect freedom of association or collective bargaining and did not effectively enforce the law. All trade and professional unions were government controlled, and none had an independent voice in its activities. The government did not permit private citizens to form independent unions. There were no labor NGOs in the country.

b. Prohibition of Forced or Compulsory Labor

The law prohibits all forms of forced or compulsory labor. The law allows for compulsory labor as a punishment for criminal offenses, requiring that convicted persons work in the place and job specified by the administration of the penal institution, potentially including private enterprises. Compulsory labor may also be applied as a punishment for libel and for violation of the established procedure for the organization of assemblies, meetings, or demonstrations.

The law provides for the investigation, prosecution, and punishment of suspected forced labor and other trafficking offenses. Resources, inspections, and remediation were inadequate. Penalties for violations, including fines of up to 2,000 manat ($570) or suspension of an employer's operations for up to three months, were inconsistently enforced and insufficient to deter violations. The government reported it conducted investigations and convicted traffickers. Construction workers in the informal sector were vulnerable to forced labor, and there was widespread use of government-compelled forced labor in the cotton industry. To meet government-imposed quotas for the cotton harvest, local authorities sometimes required university students, private-sector institution employees, soldiers, and public-sector workers to pick cotton without compensation and under threat of penalty.

Also see the Department of State's *Trafficking in Persons Report* at www.state.gov/j/tip/rls/tiprpt/.

c. Prohibition of Child Labor and Minimum Age for Employment

During the year the government amended the labor code to increase the minimum age at which a person can enter into a labor agreement/contract from 16 years of age to 18 years. A 15-year-old, however, may work four to six hours per day, up to 24 hours per week, with parental and trade union permission. The law prohibits children between the ages of 16 and 18 from working more than six hours per day, or 36 hours per week. The law also prohibits children from working overtime or between the hours of 10 p.m. and 6 a.m., and protects children from exploitation in the workplace. A presidential decree bans child labor in all sectors and states specifically that children may not participate in the cotton harvest.

Resources, inspections, and remediation were reportedly adequate to enforce the prohibitions on child labor. Penalties for violations, including fines of up to 2,000 manat ($570) or suspension of an employer's operations for up to three months, were enforced and sufficient to deter violations. The Ministry of Justice and the Prosecutor General's Office effectively enforced the section of the labor code prohibiting forced child labor.

Radio Free Europe/Radio Liberty reported that some children picked cotton to earn extra money, and there were limited reports of children working in other industries, but there were no confirmed reports of forced child labor in the cotton industry.

d. Discrimination with Respect to Employment and Occupation

The law prohibits discrimination on the basis of nationality, race, gender, origin, language, religion, disability, HIV status or other communicable diseases, political beliefs, and social status. The government did not always effectively enforce the law, which does not specify penalties for discrimination on these grounds, with the exception of disability; discrimination against disabled persons is punishable by fine ranging from 203 manat to 2,000 manat ($58 to $572) and suspension for up to three months. The law does not prohibit discrimination on the basis of age, sexual orientation, or gender identity.

Discrimination in employment and occupation on the basis of gender, language, and disability (see section 6) was widespread across all sectors of the economy and government. Certain government positions required language exams and all government positions require a family background check going back three generations. Civil society members reported that the country retained a strong cultural bias against women in positions of power and leadership, making it difficult for some women to secure managerial positions based on their gender. Although the 2013 Code on the Social Protection of the Population defined social protection policies for persons with disabilities and established quotas and work places for persons with disabilities, it was not broadly enforced. Members of the disability rights community reported that persons with disabilities were generally unable to find satisfactory employment due to unofficial discrimination. There was no information on discrimination against internal migrant workers.

e. Acceptable Conditions of Work

The minimum monthly wage in all sectors was 590 manat (approximately $170). A presidential decree raised wages by 10 percent in January.

An official estimate of the poverty-level income was not available. The standard legal workweek is 40 hours with weekends off. The law states overtime or holiday pay should be double the regular wage. Maximum overtime in a year is 120 hours and may not exceed four hours in two consecutive days. The law prohibits pregnant women, women with children up to age three, women with disabled children under age 16, and single parents with two or more children from working overtime.

The law provides a minimum of 30 days of paid annual leave for state employees, 45 days for teachers at all types of educational institutions, and 55 days for professors. The law permits newlyweds and their parents 10 days of paid leave for the preparation of weddings. Workers also receive 10 days of paid leave to carry out funeral rites and commemoration ceremonies in the event of a death of a close relative. Upon reaching age 62, citizens are entitled to an additional three days of paid leave.

The government did not set comprehensive standards for occupational health and safety. In 2013 the government reformed the labor code to provide additional benefits, including bonus pay, reduced work hours, additional leave time, and eligibility for early retirement, for work deemed hazardous. There is no state labor inspectorate. State trade unions, however, employed 14 labor inspectors, who have the right to issue improvement notices to government industries. According to the law, trade union inspectors cannot levy fines, and there are no mechanisms for enforcement of improvement notices.

The government required its workers and many private-sector employees to work 10 hours a day or a sixth day without compensation. Reports indicated many public-sector employees worked at least a half-day on Saturdays. Laws governing overtime and holiday pay were not effectively enforced. There were no defined penalties for violation of wage and hour provisions, and no state agency was designated for enforcement.

Employers did not provide construction workers and industrial workers in older factories proper protective equipment and often made these workers labor in unsafe environments. Some agricultural workers faced environmental health hazards related to the application of defoliants in preparing cotton fields for mechanical harvesting. Workers did not have the right to remove themselves from work situations that endangered their health or safety without jeopardy to their continued employment, and authorities did not protect employees in this situation. Statistics regarding work-related injuries and fatalities were not available.